DK WORKBOOKS

Computer
CODING

Author and Consultant Jon Woodcock

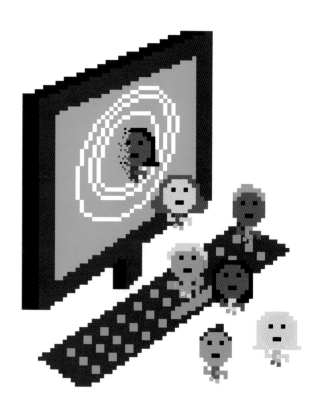

Written by
Jon Woodcock
Editor Steve Setford
Designer Peter Radcliffe
Publisher Laura Buller
Art Director & Jacket Designer Martin Wilson
Producer, Pre-Production Francesca Wardell
Producer Christine Ni
Publishing Director Sophie Mitchell
US Editor Jill Hamilton

First American Edition, 2014
Published in the United States by DK Publishing
345 Hudson Street, New York, New York 10014

15 16 17 18 10 9 8 7 6
011—256553—Aug/2014

A catalog record for this book is available
from the Library of Congress.
ISBN: 978-1-4654-2685-7

DK books are available at special discounts when
purchased in bulk for sales promotions, premiums,
fund-raising, or educational use.
For details, contact:
DK Publishing Special Markets
345 Hudson Street, New York, New York 10014
SpecialSales@dk.com

Printed and bound in China

Discover more at **www.dk.com**

Contents

Now get coding

Meet Python!

What are computer programs? Why do they matter? And what's the point in learning to create them? It might surprise you to learn that computer programs make our high-tech world what it is today.

What is a computer program?

Computers are all around us—but we often don't know they are there. They include desktop and laptop computers, but there are also computers inside our phones and tablets, in games consoles, and even in TVs, washing machines, and cars.

Computers carry out lists of instructions called programs. Video games, web-browsers, and word processors are all computer programs. More surprisingly, perhaps, building elevators, the different settings on washing machines, and how the brakes are activated on your car are controlled by computer programs too.

Why learn to program?

If you learn to create programs, you can take control of the computers around you. Become a programmer, and you'll be able to make your own games, control your own robots, and write your own apps for mobile devices. Most importantly, programming is challenging and fun, and it's good exercise for your brain!

How to make a computer program

We can't just tell a computer to "play chess"—computers don't know anything about the game. Instead, the programmer has to tell the computer everything it needs to know about chess in small, simple chunks of information. Computers also don't understand normal language—they have to be told what to do using special instructions from what's known as a programming language.

The language of programming

The instructions to a computer that tell it how to perform a certain task need to be coded in a language that's simple enough for computers to use and yet can also be understood by humans (so they can make the program). We then "run" our program so that the computer performs the task.

There are lots of different programming languages, designed to enable computers to carry out a wide range of tasks. They tend to have odd-sounding names, such as Java, C++, and Ruby.

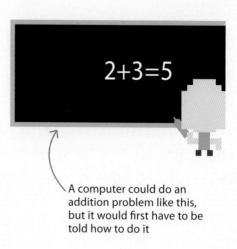

A computer could do an addition problem like this, but it would first have to be told how to do it

Python—it's not a snake!

Python is a programming language. Although it's easy to learn, it can be used to write all sorts of programs. Python is used not only in schools but also by many companies and universities around the world.

Python is designed so that its programs are easy to read and understand. It's a great first language to learn, and as you become more skilled at programming you'll be able to use it for increasingly complex projects. You'll be learning the basics of Python in this workbook, but the concepts that you'll meet are part of any programming language.

```
EasterEgg.py
IDLE    File    Edit    Format    Run    Window    Help

N = 10
for n in range(1, N + 1):
    a = 0
    for m in range(1, n + 1):
        for k in range(1, m + 1):
            print('*', end='')
        a += m
        print()
    print(n, a)
    print()
```

This is the kind of window you'll see on your computer screen when you start coding in Python

How to use this book

This book starts you off coding in Python. Each new idea is explained using examples mixed with exercises and practice sections to help you understand and remember how that part of Python works.

After you've worked though a section, it's fun and easy to try the code from the examples and exercises on your own computer. To do this, you'll first need to install Python (see pages 6–7).

Installing Python

To really understand the contents of this workbook, you'll need to install Python 3 on your computer. This will enable you to run the code in the examples and problems.

What you'll learn:
• What IDLE is
• How to install Python 3 and IDLE on a computer
• Not to use Python 2 with this book!

Using IDLE to work with Python 3

We will be using a program called IDLE, which makes using Python easier. IDLE is installed along with Python. So let's get going—install Python and start IDLE using the following instructions for your computer.

First ask permission from whoever owns the computer you're using to install Python, and ask them to help you do so—you may need them to enter administrator passwords during the installation process.

Python warning!
You might be lucky and find that Python is already installed on the computer—but check that it's Python 3, not Python 2. When you start IDLE, the number shown right after "Python" on the first line should be a 3, not a 2. The contents of this book won't work on Python 2. If in doubt, follow the instructions below to install Python 3.

Installing for Windows

Before you download Python, check which version of Windows the computer has—the 32-bit or 64-bit version. To find out, click on the "Start" button, right-click "Computer", and left-click "Properties". Then choose "System" if the option appears.

1 **Go to the Python website**
Type the address below into your Internet browser to open the Python website. Then click on "Download" in the navigation panel to open the download page.

http://www.python.org

This is the URL (web address) for Python

2 **Download Python**
Click on the latest version of Python for Windows, beginning with the number 3, which will be near the top.

• Python 3.3.3 Windows x86 MSI Installer
• Python 3.3.3 Windows x86-64 MSI Installer

Choose this if you have a 32-bit version of Windows (or if you're not sure)

Don't worry about the exact number, so long as it has a 3 at the front

Choose this if you have a 64-bit version of Windows

3 **Install it!**
The installer file will download automatically. When it finishes, double-click it to install Python. Choose "install for all users" and click "next" at each prompt, without changing the default settings.

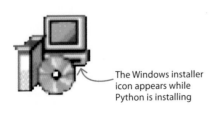

The Windows installer icon appears while Python is installing

4 **Run IDLE**
Now check that the program has installed correctly. Open the Windows "Start" menu, click on "All Programs", "Python", and then choose "IDLE".

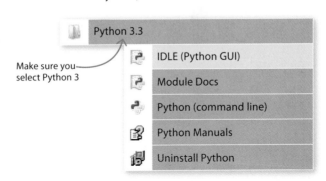

Python 3.3

Make sure you select Python 3

IDLE (Python GUI)
Module Docs
Python (command line)
Python Manuals
Uninstall Python

5 **A Python window opens**
A window like the one at right
should open up. You can now start
coding—just type into the window
after the angle brackets (>>>).

Begin typing code here

```
Python 3 Shell
IDLE    File    Edit    Shell    Debug    Window    Help

Python 3.3.3 (v3.3.3:c3896275c0f6, Nov 18 2013, 21:19:30) [MSC
v.1600 64 bit (AMD64)] on win32
Type "copyright", "credits" or "license()" for more
information.
>>>
```

Installing for Mac OS X

If you use an Apple Mac, find out which operating system it has before you install Python. You can do this by clicking on the apple icon in the top left of the screen and choosing "About This Mac" from the drop-down menu.

1 **Go to the Python link**
Type the address below into
your Internet browser to open the
Python website. Then click on
"Download" in the navigation panel
to go to the download page.

http://www.python.org

2 **Download Python**
Check which operating system
your Mac has (see above) and click on
the version that matches Python 3.
You'll be prompted to save a .dmg
file. Save it on your Mac desktop.

This version is for
newer Macs

- Python 3.3.3 Mac OS X 64-bit... (for Mac OS X 10.6 and later)

- Python 3.3.3 Mac OS X 32-bit... (for Mac OS X 10.5 and later)

Don't worry about the
exact number, so long
as it has a 3 at the front

This version runs
on most Macs

3 **Install it!**
Double-click the .dmg file.
A window will open with several
files in it, including the Python
installer file, called "Python.mpkg".
Double-click it to start the installation.

4 **Run IDLE**
During the installation process,
click "next" at each prompt to accept the default
settings. After installation ends, open the
"Applications" folder on your Mac and open the
"Python" folder (remember to make sure you select
Python 3, not Python 2). Then double-click "IDLE" to
check that the installation has worked.

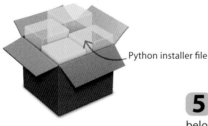

Python installer file

Python.mpkg

IDLE icon

5 **A Python window opens**
A window like the one shown
below should open. You can now
start coding—just type into the
window after the angle brackets.

```
Python 3 Shell
IDLE    File    Edit    Shell    Debug    Window    Help

Python 3.3.3 (v3.3.3:c3896275c0f6, Nov 16 2013, 23:39:35)
[GCC 4.2.1 (Apple Inc. build 5666) (dot 3)] on darwin
Type "copyright", "credits" or "license()" for more information.
>>>
```

Begin typing code here

Python and IDLE

Now that you have Python 3 and its helper program IDLE installed on your computer, it's time to try out some code. There are two ways to use Python in IDLE—both are explained here.

> **What you'll learn:**
> • How to enter Python on the computer
> • Using the IDLE shell window for instant feedback
> • Using the IDLE code window for more complex programs
> • How to use this book with a computer

Using the IDLE shell window

The easiest way to get started with Python is by using the shell window, in which any Python you type is immediately run and any output or errors are displayed. Try out the shell…

1 Start up the IDLE program by following the instructions for your type of computer given in the Installing Python section (see pages 6–7). This will open up Python's shell window.

2 The shell window shows the output (any data that the program produces) and any errors.

Python Shell 3

IDLE	File	Edit	Shell	Debug	Window	Help

```
Python 3.3.3 (v3.3.3:c3896275c0f6, Nov 16 2013, 23:39:35)
[GCC 4.2.1 (Apple Inc. build 5666) (dot 3)] on darwin
Type "copyright", "credits" or "license()" for more information.
>>>
```

Enter Python commands at the prompt

What appears here will depend on which operating system you're using

3 When you type Python commands at the prompt (>>>), Python shows the output straight away.

Python command

```
>>> print('Hello World!')
Hello World!
>>> 3 + 4
7
>>>
```

Python output

Python command

Python output

Red alert! Red text means there's something wrong!

4 If you get any messages in red mentioning the word "Error", then you've typed something Python doesn't understand—check the code in the book and retype carefully.

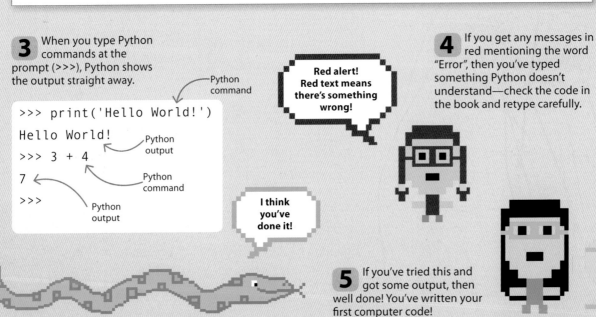

I think you've done it!

5 If you've tried this and got some output, then well done! You've written your first computer code!

Using the IDLE code window

With more complicated programs, it's easier to enter a whole program and then ask Python to run the program for you. For this, we use another window to enter the code, which in this book we'll call the code window. Try it yourself…

1 Start IDLE by following the instructions for your type of computer in the Installing Python section (see pages 6–7). You'll get the shell window. Click on the File menu at the top and select New Window.

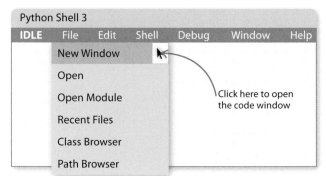

Click here to open the code window

2 A new type of window, called a code window, will appear. Enter some code in this window. For example:

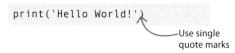

```
print('Hello World!')
```

Use single quote marks

3 We then need to save this code by selecting the File menu and choosing the "Save As" command.

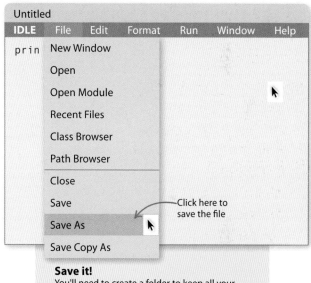

Click here to save the file

4 Now we have saved the code we can try it out. Click on the Run menu and select "Run Module".

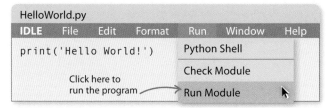

Click here to run the program

Save it!
You'll need to create a folder to keep all your program files in. Give the folder a clear name, such as "PythonCode", and agree with the person who owns the computer where to keep it. When saving a Python program, you have to give it a name. Choose a meaningful name, but avoid using names that Python uses—for example, "turtle"—which may cause problems.

5 The output appears in the shell window (not the code window).

```
>>>

Hello World!

>>>
```

6 Fantastic! You've saved your first program and run it!

7 You might get errors—popups or messages in the shell window. If so, recheck your code and try again.

Enter code ➡ Save ➡ Run

How to use this book with Python on a computer
• Follow the examples and try the exercises/problems in the book.
• Then try them on a computer (get an adult to help with this bit if you get stuck).
• The exercises in the first part of the book work best from the IDLE shell window to instantly execute (run) instructions.
• The later and longer examples and exercises work best when you use the IDLE code window to save and run code.

Robot programs

Computers can carry out complex tasks, but they aren't very clever. So every task has to be broken down into a series of very simple steps. When these steps are turned into language a computer can understand, it makes a computer program.

What you'll learn:
• How to think like a computer
• How to break a problem down into simple steps
• How to combine simple commands to complete complex tasks
• What an algorithm is
• What a computer program is

Thinking like a computer

Before you start programming a computer, you need to learn to think like one. This means dividing tasks into simple steps. To get into this way of thinking, imagine you're controlling a robot. Your task is to get this robot through a series of simple mazes. If you just say "Solve the maze!" to the robot, nothing will happen. The only instructions the robot understands are:

F = Move forward one square in the direction you are pointing.
R = Turn 90 degrees (a quarter turn) right without going anywhere.
L = Turn 90 degrees (a quarter turn) left without going anywhere.

The robot starts on the green circle and finishes on the checkered flag.

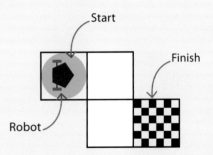

Example

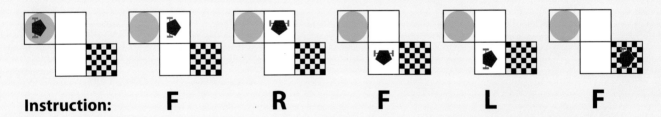

Instruction: F R F L F

Each instruction for our robot is a single step in our program. The complete program for getting our robot through the maze is "F-R-F-L-F". We can write all sorts of programs for our robot using just our three simple instructions.

Amazing algorithms!

An algorithm is a set of steps that, when followed in order, carry out a task. For example, the recipe for making a cake is an algorithm. A computer program is an algorithm written in a language that a computer can understand, so that it can perform a particular task.

Get me out of here!

Create programs to help your robot find its way through these mazes. Begin at the green circle and end at the chequered flag. The pink walls cannot be crossed, so you have to go round them. The robot is shown in its starting position and direction.

1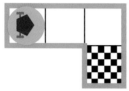
F F

2
F F R F

3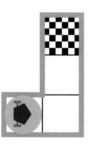
F L F F

4
F F R F R F F

5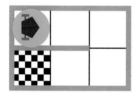
F F R F F L
F L F F R F

6
F F F F R
F F F R F
F R F L F
L F F F F
L F F R F
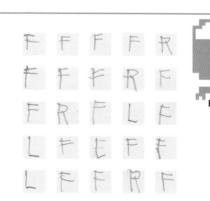

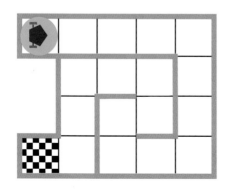
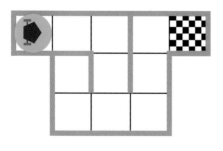

Turtle graphics

You've seen that a computer program has to be a precise set of steps. Here, you'll learn how to draw on the screen by driving another pretend robot using Python.

What you'll learn:
• What turtle graphics are
• How to write simple turtle robot control commands in Python
• How to draw shapes with Python's turtle
• How to try out Python's turtle on a computer

Turtle commands in Python

We can control an imaginary robot turtle by typing Python commands such as:

```
forward(50)
right(90)
left(90)
```
Move forward 50 steps (like the command F from page 10)
Turn right 90 degrees (like R from page 10)
Turn left 90 degrees (like L from page 10)

Each command has a name followed by a value in brackets that gives extra information about what the robot should do, such as moving a specific distance or turning a certain number of degrees. You can combine these Python commands to draw just about anything.

Drawing a square

We can use these turtle commands to draw a square.

1. Turtle in starting position

2. Move forward 100 units

```
forward(100)
```

Command is called **forward**

Number is passed as additional information to the command

This is like our F command (page 10), but it leaves a trail behind it. It moves the turtle 100 units forward.

3. Turn right 90 degrees

```
right(90)
```

Like R (page 10), it turns the turtle 90 degrees, changing its direction.

---

4. Move forward 100 units

```
forward(100)
```

This instruction tells the turtle to move 100 units forward in the new direction …

… and so on, until the turtle has drawn a square.

5. Commands to complete the square:

```
right(90)
forward(100)
right(90)
forward(100)
```

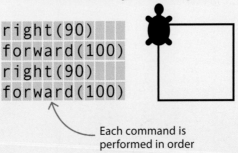

Each command is performed in order

We can vary the distances the turtle moves and the angles of its turns, or turn it the other way using `left()`, to draw any shape we want:

```
forward(150)
left(120)
forward(150)
left(120)
forward(150)
left(120)
```

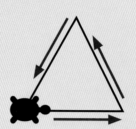

Turtle always starts pointing to the right

1 Write a code to draw this shape (each line is 100 units long):

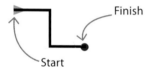

Finish

Start

2 Write a code to do the same drawing, but at half the size (so each line is only 50 units long):

Finish

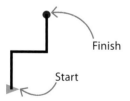

Start

3 Draw this shape simply by adding an extra command to your solution to problem 2:

Finish

Start

4 Now try drawing this shape:

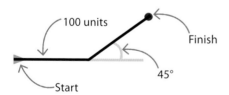

100 units

Finish

45°

Start

Try Python's turtle graphics on a computer (see pages 6–7 for installation details):

• Enter the command **from turtle import *** to load up the turtle commands into Python.
• Enter your turtle commands at the >>> prompt. The turtle graphics will appear in their own separate window.

• If you want your turtle to look like a turtle, then try the command **shape('turtle')**.
• The command **reset()** clears the drawing space. It puts the turtle in the centre of the window, facing right.

Variables

Information, or data, is the lifeblood of computers. Data comes in many forms, such as numbers, words, pictures, and music. Variables are a handy way to store data.

Variables—boxes for data

A computer program often has to store data it will need later. To do this we use variables. A variable is like a box with a name label. You can store data in the box and then find it later using the name.

Making a new variable

To create a new variable in Python we use the assignment operator (=):

Name of variable

Assignment operator

Value to store in variable

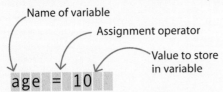

```
age = 10
```

This creates a variable called **age** that contains the value **10**.

Good names for variables

Try to choose names that describe what data the variable stores. Variable names can use any letters and numbers, although they can't start with a number. They can also use underscore (_), but no spaces or other symbols are allowed. There are a few words Python won't let you use because it's using them already, like **for** or **print**. Note that case matters: FLOWERS is a different variable than Flowers, flowers, and FloWerS.

Looking inside a variable

We can see what's in a variable using **print()**.

```
print(age)
```

Output
| 10

Changing the data in a variable

We can use the assignment operator (=) to change the value stored in a variable.

```
age = 11
print(age)
```

Output
| 11

The new assignment replaces the old value (**10**) with the new value (**11**). The old value disappears.

Copying the value of a variable

We can copy the value of a variable into another variable.

```
old_age = age
print(old_age, age)
```

Output
| 11 11

So **old_age** now holds a copy of the value of **age**, but only the value is copied. There is no connection between the variables, so if we change the value of **age** again, **old_age** keeps the value we first assigned to it.

```
age = 12
print(old_age, age)
```

Output

|11 12

You can see that **old_age** won't change until we assign it another value.

Types of data in Python

Each item of data used in Python is described as being of a particular data type. Below are a few of the simplest data types.

- Integers (type: **int**) are numbers with no decimal point. Examples: `3, 10, -2`
- Floating point numbers (type: **float**) are numbers with a decimal point. Examples: `3.1, 9.63, -4.1172, 8.0`
- Strings (type: **str**) are sequences of characters surrounded by quotes. Examples: `'Hello', 'Dave'`

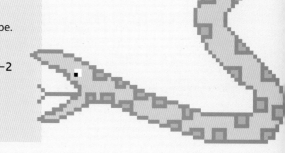

Write the Python code for these tasks:

1 a) Create a new variable called `rabbits`. **Assign the value 126 to it.**

b) **Create a new variable called** `carrots`. **Assign the value 0 to it.**

---

2 Print the contents of the variable `rabbits`.

---

3 Change the contents of the variable `rabbits` to 150, then print the value of `rabbits`.

---

4 a) Copy the value of `rabbits` into the variable `carrots`.

b) **Print the value of** `rabbits` **and** `carrots`, **using a single** `print()`.

c) **Change the value of** `rabbits` **to 250 and print the value of both** `rabbits` **and** `carrots`.

Using numbers

Computers are very good at working with numbers. Python can do all the math you'd expect—and much more besides!

Math and coding

In coding, a sum is called an expression. An expression is a combination of data and operators, and it has a value.

An expression

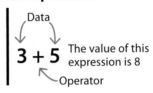

Data

3 + 5   The value of this expression is 8

Operator

Meet the operators

This table shows how the four most familiar arithmetic operations look in Python.

Operation	Operator	Example expression	Value of example expression
Add	+	13 + 6	19
Subtract	–	10 – 6	4
Multiply	* (asterisk—not a "times" symbol, ×, to avoid confusion with the letter x)	4 * 7	28
Divide	/ (not the division sign, ÷, because most keyboards don't have one)	20 / 5	4.0 ← Division always gives a **float**

Types of numbers

Remember that we've met two data types for Python numbers.
• Type `int`, such as: `3, 7, 22, 0, -6`
• Type `float`, such as: `3.1, 9.665, -4.366987, 9.0`

What data type will the answer be?

Python has rules for handling `float` and `int` numbers. If a calculation contains any numbers of type `float` (or a division), the answer will always be a `float`. If all the numbers in your calculation are of type `int` (and there are no divisions), the answer will always be an `int`.

Parentheses avoid hard-to-spot errors!

If we ask Python to compute 3 + 2 * 8, what do we get back? It could do the addition first: (3 + 2) * 8 = 40. Or it could do the multiplication first: 3 + (2 * 8) = 19. But each method gives a different answer!

Luckily, we can make it clear which one we mean by putting parentheses around what we want Python to do first. To avoid confusion, Python will always compute sums inside parentheses before doing any other sums.

Doing math with variables

We can use variables in our calculations. Let's say we have 12 rabbits:

```
rabbits = 12
```

We want to buy 3 carrots for each rabbit, so to calculate the number of carrots we need:

```
carrots = 3 * rabbits
print(carrots)
```

Output
36

Do it yourself!
You can use the IDLE shell to try Python math on your own computer.

Note that **carrots** just stores the result of the sum, not the sum itself. If we change the value of **rabbits**, we'd need to recalculate the number of carrots:

```
rabbits = 27
print(carrots)
```

Output
36

Value remains the same unless we recalculate **carrots**

---

1 Be the computer! Calculate the values of these expressions.

3 + 6   5 – 4   6 * 3   8 / 2   7 / 2

---

2 Turn these sums into Python expressions.

1 add 6   3 multiplied by 5

12 subract 8   12 divided by 4

---

3 Add parentheses to the expression 4 + 5 * 6 so that:

a) Python does the addition first

b) Python does the multiplication first

---

4 Circle all the floating point numbers.

1   7.43   6.0   –12   0   12.5   1966   –6.613   28

---

5 Circle each expression with a value of type float.

3 / 5   7.3 + 1.4   6 – 3   7 + 1   7 + 1.0
3 * 8   7.2 / 3.6   6 * 9.0   5.2 – 2.5

---

6 Write the code to put:

a) m divided by 3 into new a variable p

b) m minus 6 into new a variable q

Strings and inputs

Computers don't just deal with numbers but also letters, words, and symbols. Programmers call these strings, because they "string together" characters in order.

What you'll learn:
• What a string is
• How a program can get strings from the keyboard
• How to select parts of strings

What is a string?
We tell Python something is a string by putting it inside single quotes. In Python, strings are the data type `str`.

Dave

Cheese

Example strings:
```
'hello!'
'Dave'
'3 is the magic number!!'
'G77mk%$**3!'
'jim@abc.com'
```

The single quote marks indicate that this is a string, not a command or a variable

We can give a variable a string as a value. Here, the variable **name** has the value **Dave**:

```
name = 'Dave'
print(name)
```

Output

`Dave`

The single quotes aren't shown when you print a string

Adding strings
We can add strings together, which just makes a bigger string with the added strings in order:

```
greeting = 'Good morning ' + name
print(greeting)
```

Output

`Good morning Dave`

Getting a string from the keyboard
Python has a command `input()`, which reads what is typed at the keyboard as a string.

The string within the parentheses is the prompt

```
food = input('What is your favorite food? ')
```

This will print the question on screen (the prompt) and then wait for an answer to be typed. Once the "enter" key is hit, the string is stored in the variable food:

`What is your favorite food? cheese`

cheese is what the user types before pressing "enter"

We can then use this string:

```
print(name, 'likes', food)
```

Output

`Dave likes cheese`

Bits of strings

Python numbers the characters in a string, starting from zero:

```
run = 'Run away!'
         012345678
```

Python counts from zero, so the first character is numbered 0

Output shows characters 0, 5, and 7 from the string

We can select just a few characters from the string:

```
print(run[0], run[5], run[8])
```

Output

R w !

```
'Run away!'
 012345678
```

We can also specify a range to pick a part (or slice) of a string. We give the numbers of the first character and the number just after the last character we want:

```
print(run[4:8])
```

Output

away

Python doesn't show character 8—it always stops one character before the last number

---

1 **a) Put a string containing the word elephant in the variable** `animal`.

b) Put a string containing the word pink in a variable called `color`.

c) Make a single string by adding these two variables to make pinkelephant. Store it in the variable `dream` **and print** `dream`.

d) Change the value of `dream` **so that there's a space between the words.**

---

2 **a) Show the user the question** `What is your name?` **and put the answer he or she types into the variable** `name`.

b) Put the first letter of the entered name in a called variable `initial`.

---

3 `s = 'David James Smith'`. **Copy just the name James into the variable** `m`.

In the loop

Do you want to know how to tell your computer to do something over and over again? You'll need to discover loops!

Printing race numbers

We often use computers to do the same thing more than once. Imagine printing race numbers:

```
print('Race Number: 1')
print('Race Number: 2')
print('Race Number: 3')
```

Output
```
Race Number: 1
Race Number: 2
Race Number: 3
```

This code works fine for 3 race numbers, but imagine having to print 30,000! You'd have to type 30,000 lines of code, each with a different number—it would be very dull and you'd make mistakes. To get around this problem, computer code uses loops. Loops can run the same piece of code many times.

For loop

To print our race numbers using a loop, we enter the code below:

It's called a
`for` loop

Loop variable
keeps count

Instruction to go
around 3 times

Colon

```
for number in range(3):
    print('Race Number:', number)
```

Four-space indent shows that
`print()` is inside the loop—it's
the code that gets repeated

Print race number

Output
```
Race Number: 0
Race Number: 1
Race Number: 2
```

So the print gets run 3 times—once for each of the 3 trips through the loop. The variable **number** mentioned at the start of the **for** loop keeps count and increases by one each time through the loop—perfect for our race numbers. Notice that loops (like string and list indexes) start counting from zero, so we never get to 3. We could change 3 to 30000 and get all our race numbers printed with 2 lines of code—not 30,000.

Ranges—starts, ends, and steps

We can use the numbers in a **for** loop's **range()** to change how many times we go through the loop and how we count—what value the loop variable has on each trip through the loop.

Loop
variable

Count starts
with this
number

Ends before
this number

Counts up
in these

```
for count in range(start, end, step):
    print(count)
```

Starting on a different number

```
for count in range(1, 6):
    print(count)
```

Output | 1
2
3
4
5

The loop doesn't count all the way to the end number— it stops before 6

Counting in twos

```
for count in range(2, 11, 2):
    print(count)
```

Output | 2
4
6
8
10

Going backward

```
for count in range(5, 0, -1):
    print(count)
```

Output | 5
4
3
2
1

In `range()`, the step is assumed to be 1 if you don't specify a number. Also, `range(10)` with only one number is the same as `range(0, 10)`. After the loop has repeated the correct number of times, the program carries on to code below the loop—in other words, the next code without an indent.

1 Write code for a `for` loop that prints out the numbers 0 to 7—don't forget the indent! Use n as your loop variable for the problems on this page.

2 Change the range in your last answer so the loop prints out the numbers 1 to 12.

3 Change the range in your last answer so the loop counts to 99 in 3s. Think carefully about the start and end values of your range.

4 Code a rocket countdown that counts from 10 to 1, then prints "Blast off!"

5 Look back at the turtle graphics code (see page 12) that draws a square— can you make it shorter using a loop?

```
from turtle import *
```

Tricks with print

We've seen that we can use `print()` to display data. There are lots of other useful ways we can use the command `print()`.

What you'll learn:
• More ways to use print
• How to change what's printed between items (the separator)
• How to make all output appear on one line
• How to print tricky characters, such as `'`, and starting a new line

Hello World!

We've already learned to print…

• strings: `print('Hello World!')`

Output
| Hello World!

• values of variables:
```
a = 10
print(a)
```

Output
| 10

• more than one item using commas: `print('a is', a)`

Output
| a is 10

Separators

When you send more than one item to print, such as `print(a, b, c)`, Python puts a space called a separator between each item.

```
a = 1; b = 2; c = 3
print(a, b, c)
```

Output
| 1 2 3

Space between items

Let's change the separator by sending a different separator string to the print function, using `sep='/'` inside the print's command's brackets:

```
print(a, b, c, sep='/')
```

Output
| 1/2/3

or:

`print(a, b, c, sep='')`

Nothing in quotes

Output
| 123

Nothing between items

Hello world!

or we can use more than a single character:

```
print(a, b, c, sep=' and ')
```

Output
| 1 and 2 and 3

We can use any character or string as a separator, including commas and colons.

Ending lines

Normally `print()` starts a new line after it's printed what you've asked it to. You can change this by putting `end=' '` inside the parentheses. This tells print to put a space at the end of printing instead of starting a new line. You can use this in a `for` loop to print all your output on one line.

```
for n in range(1, 6):
    print(n, end=' ')
```

Output
| 1 2 3 4 5

All on one line

You can use any string you like with **end=**.

Tricky strings

Some strings get us into trouble in Python—for example, what if we want to put an apostrophe inside a string?

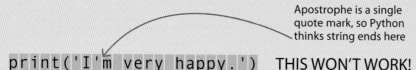

Apostrophe is a single quote mark, so Python thinks string ends here

Output
| ERROR

```
print('I'm very happy.')
```
THIS WON'T WORK!

To avoid confusing Python by using three single quotes, we put a special code character before the apostrophe. It's called an escape character.

Output
| I'm very happy.

```
print('I\'m very happy.')
```

The character combination \' tells Python to display an apostrophe, and not end the string

Another useful combination is **\n**, which inserts a new line at that point:

Output
| Hello
| Goodbye

```
print('Hello\nGoodbye')
```

---

1 Can you print these variables with a single command: x = 10; y = 20; z = 35?
Output will be: 10 20 35

---

2 Change the print command to display a comma between each of the items.
Output will be: 10 , 20 , 35

---

3 Change the print command to display a plus sign with a space either side of it between each item.
Output will be: 10 + 20 + 35

---

4 Change the print command to put a space and an equals sign at the end.
Output will be: 10 + 20 + 35 =

Lists

It's useful to be able to keep lots of information together. Python does this using a data type called a `list`.

Creating a simple list

A list can be stored in a variable, and its contents accessed and altered. Let's start by creating a list of things we need to buy:

```python
shopping = ['cherries', 'cheese', 'cream']
```

Lists use square brackets

This list of strings is now stored in a variable called **shopping**. A list keeps the items in order. We can print our shopping list:

```python
print(shopping)
```

Output | `['cherries', 'cheese', 'cream']`

I'd put cheese on my list!

Adding an item at the end of a list

We can use **append** to add a new item at the end of the list:

```python
shopping.append('banana')
print(shopping)
```

Output | `['cherries', 'cheese', 'cream', 'banana']`

List index numbers

Python gives each item in a list an index number to identify it. Index numbers always start at zero.

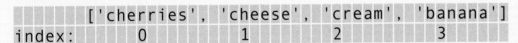

```
          ['cherries', 'cheese', 'cream', 'banana']
index:        0          1         2         3
```

Working with lists

We can use index numbers to change, retrieve, or delete an item. To retrieve the item **banana** from our shopping list:

```python
print(shopping[3])
```
Output | `banana`

Fourth item on list

For **loops and lists**

We can use a loop to access list items in order:

Loop variable takes value of each list item in turn

```python
for item in shopping:
    print(item)
```

Output

```
cherries
cheese
cream
banana
```

Task	Command	List contents after command executed
Basic list	Index	['cherries', 'cheese', 'cream', 'banana']
1 Change an item	`shopping[3] = 'custard'`	['cherries', 'cheese', 'cream', 'custard']
2 Delete an item	`del shopping[3]` — Removes item and closes the gap	['cherries', 'cheese', 'cream']
3 Insert an item	`shopping.insert(1, 'oranges')` — Inserts new item at given index and shuffles the rest of the items along	['cherries', 'oranges', 'cheese', 'cream']

1 Create a list containing the names of the colors red, green, and blue as strings and store it in a variable called `colors`.

2 Write the code to display the whole `colors` list using the `print()` function.

3 Change the print code to display just the second item on the list (green).

4 How could we change the first entry in `colors` from red to pink after it has been created?

5 Delete the third entry on the list.

6 Add `purple` at the end of the list.

7 Insert `yellow` at the start of the list (remember: the first list item has index 0).

True or False?

Python makes decisions using questions, called Boolean expressions, with yes/no answers. Their value is either True or False.

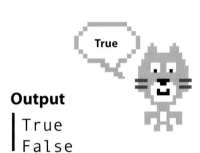

What you'll learn:
• Boolean expressions are either True or False
• There are many different comparison operators to compare data
• Comparison operators work for numbers and strings
• Boolean expressions can be joined using the logical operators **and** and **or**

Boolean expressions

A Boolean expression uses a comparison operator to compare two pieces of data.

Data—in this case, a variable

Data

```
age < 18
```

Comparison operator—in this case, "less than"

For example, the value of the expression above is either True or False: any value of **age** of 17 or below makes the expression True; if **age** is 18 and above, it is False.

You can print out the value of a Boolean expression:

```
print(3 > 2)
print(3 < 2)
```

Output

```
True
False
```

True

False

True and False have their own data type, called type **bool**, (short for Boolean). Note that both start with capital letters.

Comparison operators

Numbers can be compared in Python using these operators:

Comparison operator	Example Boolean expression	Value (if age has value 10)
Equal to	age == 10	True
Greater than	age > 10	False
Less than	age < 10	False
Greater than or equal to	age >= 10	True
Less than or equal to	age <= 10	True
Not equal to	age != 10	False

Note that "is equal to" uses TWO equals signs, to avoid confusion with the assignment operator (just one equals sign)

Comparing strings

Strings can also be compared, but their contents must be exactly the same for them to be equal—even spaces and capital letters have to be identical.

The capital "A" and lower case "a" don't match

The two strings are not the same (different names)

```
'Amy' == 'amy'      False
'Amy' == ' Amy'     False
'Amy' != 'Beth'     True
'10' == 10          False
```

Extra space in second piece of data

String types are never equal to number types

Logical operators

You can combine two Boolean expression using Python's **and** and **or** operators to make more specific tests:

True only if both expressions are True
(expression one and expression two)
—so age must be 11 to 17

True if either (or both) parts are True
(expression one or expression two)—
so for 10 and under, or 18 and over

```
age > 10 and age < 18
```

```
age <= 10 or age >= 18
```

1 Are the following Boolean expressions True (T) or False (F)?
Variable values: a = 10 ; b = 3

1 < 2	6 == 6	9 != 10	8 <= 4	4 >= 4
a == 3	a > 3	b != 3	b >= 3	b >= 0
a == b	a != b	a < b	a >= (b + 6)	a <= (b + 6)

2 What are the Python Boolean expressions for these statements?

a) c **is less than 1000**

b) d **is not equal to** a

c) d **is equal to 6**

d) c **is greater than or equal to 12**

e) (c **add** d) **is less than or equal to 10**

3 Here are some more Boolean expressions to work out, but this time
they include the logic operators **and** and **or**.
Variable values: a = 10 ; b = 3

a == 10 and b == 3	a == 10 and b > 3	a != 10 and b >= 3
a >= 5 and b <= 5	a > 5 and a < 15	a == 4 or a == 10
a > 0 or b > 0	b == a or a < 10	a > b or b != 100

4 Write Boolean expressions that are True if:

a) **both** x **and** y **are less than 5**

b) **either** x **is greater than 1,000 or** y **is 250 (or both)**

Branches

We've seen how to make True/False decisions using Boolean expressions. Now we'll see how to use them in a program to choose what a program does.

What is a branch of a program?

With a branch, different code gets run depending on whether a condition (a Boolean expression) is True or False.

`if` ("do or skip")

The simplest branch in Python runs a block of code if a Boolean expression is True but skips it if the expression is False. Called an `if` statement, it can be read as: "if this condition is True, do the instructions in this block of code".

```
if age < 18:
    print ('No children')
```

Block of code inside `if` is indented four spaces

If condition is True, then print this message

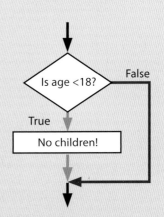

This flowchart shows that the `if` code has two branches—one that prints a message and another that skips printing the message

`if-else` ("do this, else do that")

A more complex branch can be created using `if` and `else`. It runs one block of code if a Boolean expression is True but a different block if it's False. It can be read as: "if this condition is True then do the instructions in this block of code, else do these instructions".

This means "get password from keyboard"

```
password = input('Enter Password: ')
if password == 'swordfish':
    print('Password accepted')
else:
    print('Intruder alert!')
print('Have a nice day!')
```

If password correct, print this message

This has no indent, so it isn't part of the `if-else` and is always printed

If password incorrect, print this message

Password entered	Output
swordfish	Password accepted Have a nice day!

Password entered	Output
toothbrush	Intruder alert! Have a nice day!

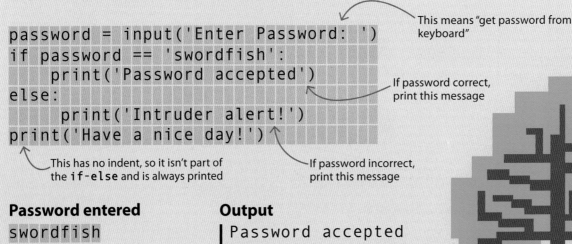

This flowchart shows that the **if-else** code has two branches—each prints a different message (the "Have a nice day!" message is outside the **if-else**, so it is always printed)

```
                        Password
                        correct?
          True                          False

   Password accepted              Intruder alert!

                  Have a nice day!
```

Do it yourself!

Try these examples on the computer, but use the code window (see pages 8–9). If you run them from the command line in the shell, you'll be likely to keep making mistakes and it will become frustrating.

1 Complete the code below to print "Good morning!", but only if Nicola is the name entered on the keyboard.

```
name = input('Enter your name: ')
```

2 Complete the code below to say "Have a cake!" if cake is entered, but offer a cookie if anything else is entered.

```
food = input('Favorite food? ')
```

3 What could you add to the code above to offer everyone a cup of tea regardless of their food preference?

4 What will be the output of the program below?

```
for n in range(1000):
    if n == 3:
        print(n)
```

Output:

While loops

For **loops are useful if you know how many times you want to do something. But if you want to keep on going until something specific happens, you need a** `while` **loop.**

What you'll learn:
• What a `while` loop is
• How to use a `while` loop
• How to make a `while` loop go on forever!
• How to escape from a `while` loop that just won't stop!

While **loops**

A `while` loop checks a condition at the top of a block of code and repeats the block only while the condition remains True. The loop ends once the condition is False. The block of code inside the loop is indented.

Guessing game

We can use a `while` loop to make a simple game to guess the name of an animal. The `while` loop keeps repeating, inviting the player to type in his or her guess, until the correct animal name is entered. The loop then ends and the player is told that he or she has won.

```
print('Guess the animal!')
guess = ''
answer = 'elephant'
while guess != answer:
    guess = input('Guess? ')
print('Correct!')
```

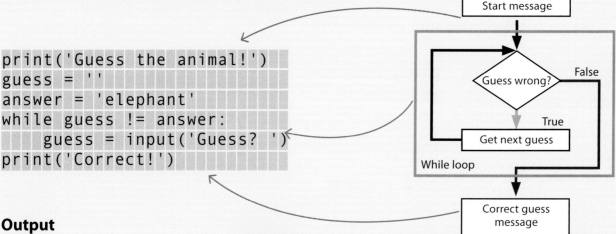

Start message

Guess wrong? — False

True

Get next guess

While loop

Correct guess message

Output

```
Guess the animal!
Guess? lion
Guess? parrot
Guess? elephant
Correct!
```

The player types in an animal name and then presses "enter"

This is a flowchart of the guessing game—confusingly, the `while` loop condition `guess != answer` is True when we guess wrong and False when we guess right!

Is it me?

Counting up

We can use a variable to count how many times we go around a `while` loop. To increase our counter by one, we use: **a = a + 1**. We need to do this so often in coding that there is a short version—it can also be written as **a += 1**.

Using this type of loop, we can write code to print the numbers 1 to 5:

```
a = 0
while a < 5:
    a = a + 1
    print(a)
```

Output

1
2
3
4
5

The loop repeats while **a** is less than 5—once **a** gets to 5, the loop is complete

Infinite loops—`while True`

With a `while` loop, we can even make loops that never stop by replacing the Boolean expression with the value True. The value False never occurs (which would end the loop), and so the `while` loop goes on forever!

```
while True:
    print('Python is cool!')
```

Do it yourself!

Run these examples from the code window (see pages 8–9). If you get stuck in a loop, go to the shell window and hold the CTRL (control) key down while pressing the C key. This should stop the loop.

---

1 Fill in the missing lines of code to make this counting program print 1 to 12.

```
a = 0


        print(a)
```

---

2 Change the counting program above so that it will count up from one forever.

---

3 Enter the missing line so the program will keep asking for names until Ranjeev arrives and then greet him.

```
name = ''

    name = input('Enter your name: ')
print('Hello Ranjeev!')
```

Functions

Some code is so useful that we want to reuse it. To avoid typing this code more than once, we turn it into a "function".

What is a function?

A function is a block of code that's been given a name. We can then use that code in a program by just including the function's name. Sometimes we pass data to a function, and sometimes a function gives data back to us.

Functions we've already met

We've already used some of Python's built-in functions without realizing:

```
print(a, b, c)
```

We pass data to the function to be displayed

Function name

```
name = input('What is your name?')
```

The function gives us back a string

Function name

We pass the prompt to the function

Hello! What is your name?

All the turtle commands (see pages 12–13) are functions, such as `forward(100)`, `right(90)`, and so on.

Making our own functions

We can create and use our own functions. First we define the function using the keyword **def** to tell Python not to run any of the instructions. It just stores the code with the name **draw_square** to be used later.

Short for "define"

Name of function

Block of instructions inside function (indented)

Variable to hold data passed into function

Size data used here

```
def draw_square(size):
    for n in range(4):
        forward(size)
        right(90)
```

To run the instructions inside the function, we just use its name followed by the size of the square in brackets.

```
draw_square(50)
draw_square(100)
```

Size data passed to function

Output

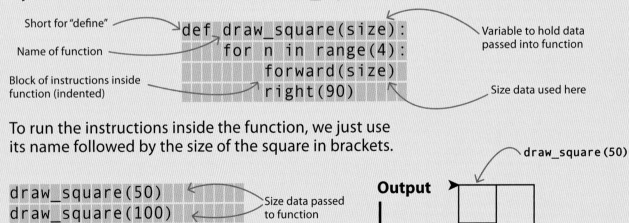

draw_square(50)

draw_square(100)

When Python sees a function name, it just replaces the name with all the code from the function definition and runs it. Using a function is also known as calling it.

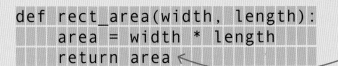

Getting data back from a function

Functions can send data back to the code that called them using the command **return**. The function below calculates the area of a rectangle:

```python
def rect_area(width, length):
    area = width * length
    return area
```

Sends the number back to the main program

We can print the data returned by the function:

```python
print(rect_area(10, 5))
```

Output

| 50

Do it yourself!

To try out functions on a computer, use the IDLE code window (see pages 8–9). And don't forget that you'll need to type **from turtle import** * before you can use the turtle.

---

1 a) Define a function called greeting that prints "Hello" followed by a name.

b) How would you run this function in Python to say hello to Dave?

---

2 An ice cream company has written a function that takes ice cream flavor as input and returns the price as output:

```python
def price(flavor):
    if flavor == 'chocolate':
        cost = 1.99
    else:
        cost = 2.49
    return cost
```

What would these outputs be?   Output:

a) `print(price('banana'))`

b) `print(price('chocolate'))`

c) `print(price('vanilla'))`

---

3 Can you write a function called draw_triangle that would draw a triangle?

```python
def draw_triangle(size):
```

Solutions

Time to check your answers! If your code doesn't match what's here, make sure you understand the solution given and then try both versions out on a computer.

Things to check:
• Do symbols, spaces, and capitals match?
• Same number of spaces before any text (indents)?
• Are all the Python words spelled correctly?

pages 10–11 Robot programs

1 F F

2 F F R F

3 F L F F

4 F F R R F R F F

5 F F R F F L
F L F F R F

6 F F F F R
F F F R F
F R F R F
L F L F F
L F F R F

pages 12–13 Turtles

1

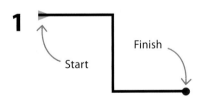

Finish
Start

```
forward(100)
right(90)
forward(100)
left(90)
forward(100)
```

2

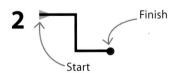

Finish
Start

```
forward(50)
right(90)
forward(50)
left(90)
forward(50)
```

3

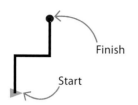

```
left(90)
forward(50)
right(90)
forward(50)
left(90)
forward(50)
```

4

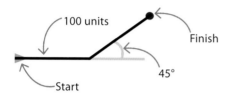

```
forward(100)
left(45)
forward(100)
```

pages 14–15 Variables

1 a) `rabbits = 126`
   b) `carrots = 0`

2 `print(rabbits)`

3 `rabbits = 150`
   `print(rabbits)`

4 a) `carrots = rabbits`
   b) `print(rabbits, carrots)`
   c) `rabbits = 250`
      `print(rabbits, carrots)`

pages 16–17 Using numbers

1 3 + 6 9   5 – 4 1   6 * 3 18   8 / 2 4.0   7 / 2 3.5

2

1 add 6	1 + 6	3 multiplied by 5	3 * 5
12 subract 8	12 – 8	12 divided by 4	12 / 4

3 a) `(4 + 5) * 6`   b) `4 + (5 * 6)`

4 1 7.43 6.0 -12 0 12.5 1966 -6.613 28

5 3 / 5   7.3 + 1.4   6 - 3   7 + 1   7 + 1.0
3 * 8   7.2 / 3.6   6 * 9.0   5.2 - 2.5

6 a) `p = m / 3`   b) `q = m - 6`

pages 18–19 Strings and inputs

1 a) `animal = 'elephant'`
b) `color = 'pink'`
c) `dream = color + animal`
`print(dream)`
d) `dream = color + ' ' + animal`

2 a) `name = input('What is your name?')`
b) `initial = name[0]`

3 `m = s[6:11]`

pages 20–21 In the loop

1
```
for n in range(8):
    print(n)
```

2
```
for n in range(1, 13):
    print(n)
```

3
```
for n in range(3, 100, 3):
    print(n)
```

4
```
for count in range(10, 0, -1):
    print(count)
print('Blast off!')
```

5
```
from turtle import *
for n in range(4):
    forward(100)
    right(90)
```

pages 22–23 Tricks with print

1
```
print(x, y, z)
```

2
```
print(x, y, z, sep=',')
```

3
```
print(x, y, z, sep=' + ')
```

4
```
print(x, y, z, sep=' + ', end=' =')
```

pages 24–25 Lists

1
```
colors = ['red', 'green', 'blue']
```

2
```
print(colors)
```

3
```
print(colors[1])
```

4
```
colors[0] = 'pink'
```

5
```
del colors[2]
```

```
6 colors.append('purple')
```

```
7 colors.insert(0, 'yellow')
```

pages 26–27 True or False?

1

1 < 2 T	6 == 6 T	9 != 10 T	8 <= 4 F	4 >= 4 T
a == 3 F	a > 3 T	b != 3 F	b >= 3 T	b >= 0 T
a == b F	a != b T	a < b F	a >= (b + 6) T	a <= (b + 6) F

2 a) c < 1000   b) d != a   c) d == 6

d) c >= 12   e) (c + d) <= 10

3

a == 10 and b == 3 T	a == 10 and b > 3 F	a != 10 and b >= 3 F
a >= 5 and b <= 5 T	a > 5 and a < 15 T	a == 4 or a == 10 T
a > 0 or b > 0 T	b == a or a < 10 F	a > b or b != 100 T

4 a) x < 5 and y < 5   b) x > 1000 or y == 250

pages 28–29 Branches

1
```
name = input('Enter your name: ')
if name == 'Nicola':
    print('Good morning!')
```

2
```
food = input('Favorite food? ')
if food == 'cake':
    print('Have a cake!')
else:
    print('Have a cookie!')
```

3
```
print('Have a cup of tea!')
```

4 Output: 3

pages 30–31 While loops

1
```
a = 0
while a < 12:
    a = a + 1
    print(a)
```

2
```
a = 0
while True:
    a = a + 1
    print(a)
```

3
```
name = ''
while name != 'Ranjeev':
    name = input('Enter your name: ')
print('Hello Ranjeev!')
```

pages 32–33 Functions

1 a)
```
def greeting(name):
    print('Hello', name)
```
b)
```
greeting('Dave')
```

2 a) 2.49   b) 1.99   c) 2.49

3
```
def draw_triangle(size):
        for n in range(3):
        forward(size)
        left(120)
```

There are many ways to draw a triangle—this is just one, and you may have a different method. Try yours on a computer to check, but don't forget to type **from turtle import *** first.

Glossary

algorithm
A set of step-by-step instructions that describes how to perform a particular task. A computer program is a type of algorithm.

Boolean expression
A question with only two possible answers, such as "True" and "False".

branch
A point in a program where two different options are available to choose from.

call
To use a function in a program.

code block
Code that belongs together, often inside a branch or loop.

data
Information, such as text, symbols, and numerical values.

expression
A piece of code that has a value, such as 3 + 5.

float
A number with a decimal point in it.

function
A piece of code that does part of a larger task.

indent
Spaces (usually in groups of four) before code lines that define a code block.

index number
A number assigned to an item in a list. In Python, the index number of the first item will be 0, the second item 1, and so on.

input
Data that is entered into a computer; for example, from a microphone, keyboard, or mouse.

integer
A whole number, positive or negative, that does not contain a decimal point and that is not written as a fraction.

loop
Part of a program that repeats itself, to prevent the need for the same piece of code to be typed out multiple times.

module
A section of code that performs a single part of an overall program.

operating system (OS)
A computer's operating system provides the basis for other programs to run.

operator
A symbol that performs a specific function: for example, + (add) or – (subtract).

output
Data produced by a computer program and viewed by the user.

program
A set of instructions that a computer follows in order to complete a task.

programming language
A language that is used to give instructions to a computer.

run
The command to start a program.

shell
Enables code to be entered that is immediately run.

string
A series of characters (numbers, letters, or symbols).

URL
A web address.

variable
A named place where you can store information that can be changed.

Note for parents

Learning to code is exciting, but it can be frustrating if things just aren't adding up. Why not work through this book yourself? You'll pick up some idea of what computer programming is all about, putting you in a great position to help your child if he or she gets stuck. If you have access to a computer, help your child install Python on it—it's free. Trying code on a computer makes learning fun, and it helps with understanding problems and spotting errors. Happy coding!